Top Rank Local

Guide To Google Local

Steve Marineau

Contents

Top Rank Local

Guide To Google Local

Introduction

A few years ago, at the 2007 Strategic Advertising Summit, Microsoft mogul, Bill Gates, predicted yellow pages usage would drop to near zero by the year 2012 for people under the age of 50. Gates' prediction seems to be coming true as the yellow pages are beginning to see double digit declines in advertising sales, as their former users are now turning to a faster, friendlier and easier way to find local businesses—the Internet.

And while the Internet is the bane of the yellow pages' demise, with a 72.11% market-strangling hold on Internet searches, it is Google that is leading the way.

Simply put, Google has become the new "yellow pages." When you compare their market-dominating 72.11% of all Internet searches to their nearest competitor, Yahoo, with an unremarkable 14.57% of Internet searches, the case is made that *every* local business should concentrate *all* their Internet marketing efforts on Google and Google alone.

Let's face it. If your business does not show up on Google, you are basically invisible to the world. And, if your business can't be found on the first two pages of Google, you (almost) don't exist because 83% of Google searches do not make it past the bottom of Google's second page.

This book will show you how to dominate your local competition with a high ranked, fully optimized listing in the prominent Google Places/Google Maps search engine results.

This book will walk you through the steps needed to optimize your Google Places listing through several simple techniques that work together to create an overall, competition-crushing strategy. The combination of these techniques is greater as a whole than is the sum of its parts...and while you can surely skip some of the seemingly small techniques that make up part of this strategy, it will subtract from the dominance you gain by employing all of the steps together.

Forget Traditional SEO

Traditional SEO is costly and very time consuming...and definitely n*ot* where local businesses need to spend their time (or money). Traditional SEO is a moving target that changes dramatically all the time, literally shaking things up and turning the search results upside down every six months or so.

If you own a business and that business relies on a customer base in your local area, then it's time to ditch traditional thinking and join the Local Search revolution.

Take a look at these stats:

- 73% of all online activity is related to local content *(Google)*

- 66% of Americans use the Internet to find local businesses *(Comscore)*

- 54% of Americans have replaced their phone books (yellow pages) with Internet searches *(Comscore)*

- 82% of local searchers follow up with their search by phone call and/or walk-in *(TMP / Comscore)*

- 43% of search engine users are seeking a local merchant with the intent of buying in their local area

Local Search is the Answer

As a local business, you have a huge, wide-open opportunity to dominate your local competition by getting a free, prominent listing at the top of Google, using Google's local search features. Google has spent a large investment on becoming the most relevant search engine to its users, as Google understands that if you live in Las Vegas and you do a search for pizza, they know you want a pizza place in Las Vegas—not in Detroit.

This book is the ultimate secret weapon for local businesses to climb to the top of Google search results in their area. Forget about traditional SEO and expensive pay-per-click (PPC) advertising. Local Search is king...and getting your business listed on top of Google's local search features is absolutely free, making your investment into this book a complete "no-brainer."

Understand that the information I share in this book is the same information that I follow (step-by step) for my clients, who happily pay me $599 + monthly maintenance to keep their business at the top of Google's search results...and it's the exact same information I share in my marketing seminars.

Nothing is left out.

The book you hold in your hands was not written to sing the praises of local search, but instead, it was written to help you dominate your competition in your local area through local search using step-by-step, actionable methods.

Simply put...if you can follow step-by-step instructions, this book will teach you how to open the virtual floodgates of more business through new leads, increased sales, more visibility and additional customers.

Top Rank Local

Chapter 1

WHAT IS LOCAL SEARCH?

You have likely noticed recently that when you do a search on Google, often times your search results include a local area map with several local business listings next to it. These listings are easily identified because they contain prominent map markers next to each of those listings. These listings are also easily noticed because Google places them at the very top of the search results.

So just how does Google determine whether or not a search has local intent?

1. The searcher uses geographic modifiers: instead of a search for "plumber," the search includes a specific location to specify the location for which they are seeking a plumber: "Detroit plumber" or "plumber in Detroit."

2. Google uses your IP to determine your location and returns results based on their estimate of your location coupled with what they determine to be a query with local intent.

This happens when Google identifies your search as originating from a specific place (or a specific place is made as part of the specified search) and that search includes a Google local search category for that geographic area. These results come from the Google Maps database.

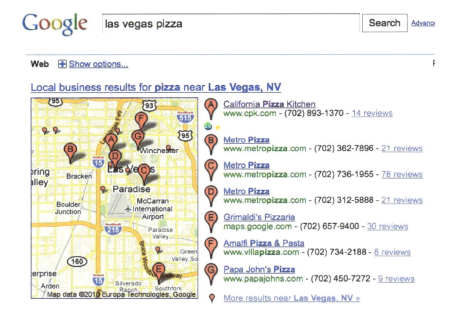

As you can see on the screenshot, I did a search for a "place" that included a "business category" recognized by Google. Google, in turn, returned relevant, local businesses listings relating to my search. More importantly, these results are at the very top of the search results!

Studies have shown over and over again that being at the top of Google correlates with more traffic, more exposure, more authority and more business. And if you own a local business, this is where you want to be. In the days when the yellow pages were the dominating "go to" source for finding local businesses, this top Google maps listing is the equivalent to a full color, full page listing.

Local search can best be described as any *online* search that takes the place of a traditional search involving the local phonebook's yellow pages. Local search is often categorized as a search being made with the intention on finding something (business, product, service) in a specific geographic. More specifically, local search can be identified by searching online for a transaction that will occur offline in one's local area.

More simply put, if you live in San Diego and you do an online search for a plumber or a pizza, the search engines understand that you want to find a plumber or pizza in the San Diego area—not in Detroit! And because the search engines know where you are (using your IP address) they can now dish out the most relevant information for your search term.

In an effort to provide the most relevant information to you, Local Search has become of great importance to the search engines. Here's why:

- According to Google, 73% of all online activity is related to local content.
- 1/3 of mobile search is locally based (Google).
- According to ComScore, 66% of Americans use the Internet to find local businesses.
- ComScore also reported that 54% of Americans have replaced the phonebook with the Internet for their local needs and that 82% of thee people follow up with a phone call or a walk-in to the business they found through local search.

Quite simply, the name of the game for the search engines is RELEVANCY. And the search engine that can be the most relevant will likely be the most used search engine...and where the eyeballs go, so does the advertising dollars.

Needless to say, over the past few years Google has become and remained the most dominant search engine on the planet. And I would argue that for no other reason than the simple fact that Google returns the most relevant information for any given search term.

The biggest concern of Google is to be the most relevant search engine to their users. This comes first to Google. Being the most relevant makes Google the "go to" search engine on the planet. Being the "go to" search engine means more customers, which in turn, makes them the "go to" source for advertisers.

I have seen Google end people's ability to support their families because these people tried to "out-think" or "out smart" Google, in an attempt to make Google see their website or advertisement as "relevant" when it really was not. Google takes no nonsense from suspected scammers who try to "mess" with their system.

The point I am trying to make is that Google strives first to be the most relevant. Making money comes next (naturally) after being the most relevant. For purposes of this book, you need to think "relevance" first—just as Google does. When you first try to be the most relevant to your customers, Google will reward you with higher rankings.

As I mentioned in the Introduction of this book, Google commands an incredible 72.11% market share of Internet searches. And while Google continues to gain market share, its biggest competitors continue to lose their share of the search market at double-digit rates. And it is because of these statistics that this book will focus on getting your business at the top of Google—specifically Google Places/Google Local Maps.

Top Rank Local

Chapter 2

Google Places

Google Places is a revolutionary and totally free service that can literally catapult a small, local business from obscurity to insane profitability almost overnight. By taking advantage of a Google Places listing, you can highlight your business' products and services and place your information in front of thousands of local customers who are searching for your particular type of business in your particular local area via Google.com.

Not only will a listing on Google Places make your business stand out among dozens (sometimes hundreds) of local competitors, you will also get to tell potential customers a little bit about your business, where your competition is unable to.

Because Google Local is relatively new, many businesses do not know about it and because of that, your competition probably doesn't know about it either! Right now, you have in your hands the ultimate "secret weapon" to gaining a stronghold in your local market—a weapon to not only getting a free, Google Places listing for your business, but inside tips, tricks and secrets to securing a front page listing for your business so that your potential customers are finding you—not your competition—when they conduct a Google search for your particular products and services in your area.

Although the SEO "experts" like to make you believe SEO is a highly complex and technical field, I can tell you that it's not. In fact, in recent years, SEO has become a lot easier because instead of trying to optimize for several different search engines, you now only have to optimize for one: Google.

Love them or hate them, Google rules the Internet with over 280 million unique searches a day, coupled with a 72% + market share of Internet searches. With that kind of action, to me it makes sense to focus all of my SEO energy on only Google.

The purpose of this book is to show you how to claim your Google Places listing and then how to optimize that listing so that you—not your competition—is found first when your customers look for your products and services on Google.

In April 2009, Google announced that Local Search would start to show up more regularly in the "regular" search engine results pages, and since then, Google has delivered. Now, when you type in "plumber" or "pizza," Google serves up prominent, top of the page local listings that are relevant to your search terms.

Prior to Google Local, many businesses paid a fortune on

Pay Per Click (PPC) ads to promote their businesses locally. Since Google Places (formerly Google Local Business Center) came on scene, however, online advertising costs for local businesses were able to be dramatically minimized by replacing PPC with a prominent Google Places listing. In my opinion, a Google Places listing is a much more prominent listing for those searching for local businesses than is their paid advertisement counterparts (on the right side of the Google page). Additionally, Google Places listings, being free, gave many local businesses an opportunity to compete with their deep-pocketed competitors who could afford to pay for expensive PPC ads.

When your business is listed in Google Places, it will show

up on the map feature when a local searcher (in your area) does a search for your business' products and/or services. As you can see in the photo, the Google Map listing (local business results) is very bold and they stand out like a colorful "sore thumb" on the Google search results.

On April 20th 2010, Google Local Business Center made another major move and became Google Places. Here's an excerpt from the official Google Blog, announcing the change:

Introducing Google Places
4/20/2010 05:00:00 AM

Today the Local Business Center is becoming Google Places. Why? Millions of people use Google every day to find places in the real world, and we want to better connect Place Pages — the way that businesses are being found today — with the tool that enables business owners to manage their presence on Google.

We launched Place Pages last September for more than 50 million places around the world to help people make more informed decisions about where to go, from restaurants and hotels to dry cleaners and bike shops, as well as non-business places like museums, schools and parks. Place Pages connect people to information from the best sources across the web, displaying photos, reviews and essential facts, as well as real-time updates and offers from business owners.

Google Places is more than just a name change. Instead, Google Places offer more tools to local business owners to increase their visibility online. These new tools include the following:

- Service Areas: If you travel to serve businesses, you can now include your service areas on your Google Places page. Additionally, if you operate without a storefront, you can now privatize your business address, which was not allowed in the past.

- New Simple Ways to Advertise: For $25 a month, Google now allows you to add tags to make your listing stand out on Google.com and on Google Maps.

- Free Photo Shoots: Google now offers a free photo shoot service, where Google photographers come to your business to take interior shots for you to include on your Google Places listing.

- Customized QR Codes: Google will now create a custom QR code that is unique to your business. This code can be placed on business cards and other marketing material. These can be scanned by a smartphone which can take the customer directly to your Google Places page.

- Real Time Updates: You can now update your Google Places page and have those updates appear instantly on Google.

- Personalized Dashboard: Google provides your Google Places page with customized information collected through search. This includes providing data to you that tells you how many visitors visited your listing and what search terms they used to get there.

Chapter 3

Ranking Considerations

The information in this chapter has not been officially verified, as Google keeps tightlipped about their algorithms and the way they operate. This information is, however, quite accurate based on my testing, research and study.

As mentioned before, your business will benefit by being relevant in Google's eyes. The more relevant your business appears—the better rankings your business will get on Google Places. The key to this book is to show you what makes your business more relevant to Google.

Trust is a major factor that Google takes into consideration when ranking your business. So, the likely question that comes to mind is, how do you go about gaining Google's trust.

When you claim your business' listing on Google Places, you go through either a telephone or mail verification. This must be done as your first step in gaining Google's trust. But while this is a step in the right direction, it is not going to give you automatic credit above your competition. You need to do more.

Business Data: if your business is not on Google Places but can be found elsewhere across the Internet, having the same or similar information about your business, Google will assign your business more trust. This includes documents that may be found on the Internet regarding your business: US Patent Application 20060149800, which is assigned to Google, demonstrates this:

> Abstract: A system determines documents that are associated with a location, identifies a group of signals associated with each of the documents, and determines authoritativeness of the documents for the location based on the signals.

Business Website: A website is not required to be listed on Google Places, but having a locally based website with search terms that are locally based for your business will surely factor in ranking your business on Google Places.

Other Directories: Being listed in vertical, local, top tier and 2nd tier directories will be a major factor in Google's trust in your business. With listings in other directories, Google's trust in you will be greatly enhanced, as you will appear more likely to be a "real" business.

Reviews: It is hard to determine how much of a role reviews play in ranking your local business in Google Places, but reviews do play a factor. In my experience, the more reviews you have, the more trust Google will give you. This trust seems to relate to ranking as well.

Citations: citations are mentions about your business on other websites. In traditional SEO, to rank higher in the search engines, it is imperative to have links that link back to your website. The more quality, relevant links you have linking to your website—the higher you will rank. With local search, citations take the place of links.

There is more to creating relevant Google Place listings and in further chapters; we will address all of those factors.

Top Rank Local

Chapter 4

Claiming Your Google

Maps/Places Listing

Before you do anything else, you need to find out if your business has already been claimed on Google Places. This is something you or someone in your business would have to have done because it does require you to go through a confirmation process. Until recently, Google only allowed confirmation by mail. But now, they offer instant verification via callback service right to the telephone number you select.

Understand that your business may be able to be found on Google, but that does not mean the same as being "listed" with Google Places. The fact that you can do a search for your business name and see 10,000 results showing up that contain your business name, does not mean your business has been _claimed_. Many make this mistake and tell me, "oh, my business is already on Google", when in fact, it is not listed with Google Places.

So, let's see if your business has been claimed...

Here's the method I use for all my clients and my own business as well. It's a quick and easy way to see if your business has been claimed or not for a few of the major directories. It even provides you with a score relative to your business on the Internet in terms of being officially listed or "claimed" in those directories.

Simply go to this website: http://www.getlisted.org where you will find a screen similar to this:

As you can see, this site is pretty self-explanatory. All you need to do to see if your business has been claimed is to type in your business name and the zip code to where your business is physically located.

In the example, I randomly typed in "Beverly Hills Plastic Surgery" with a zip code of "90210." As you can see, a business was found under this name. Also, as you can see, this cosmetic surgery business has not claimed their Google Local listing (nor Yahoo, Bing, etc). This particular Plastic Surgery Business is leaving a great deal of money on the table by not having their business listing claimed.

Also, you will see that getlisted.org gives you a "listing score." In this case, getlisted.org assigned "Beverly Hills Plastic Surgery" a score of "0%" because the business has failed to claim a listing online.

Keep in mind that the higher the score, the better for your business as it is more likely to show up when people in your area are searching for your products and services.

This again goes to show you that your business may be found on Google (this one shows the business address, phone and website) but not be listed in Google Local or Google Maps.

This means that when someone in the Beverly Hills area types "plastic surgery" or similar related search terms like "breast augmentation," "liposuction" etc, this business is not as likely to show up in Google Local/Google Maps.

Here's a look at the front page of Google when I type in "Beverly Hills Plastic Surgery." Also remember that if I were actually on my computer in Beverly Hills, Google would know my location and would show these same results if I only typed in "Plastic Surgeon."

If our particular cosmetic surgeon has a copy of this book, he would easily be able to dominate this Google Map listing by knowing the secrets that you are about to learn.

Now, we will walk through getting listed in step-by-step fashion using a fictional business name.

Step 1: go to getlisted.org and enter your business name and zip code and click the "Check My Listings" box.

Step 2: once we click the "Check My Listings" box, we come up with this:

Step 3: From here, we will click "Add your business listing" that appears on the Google logo at the top of the page.

Note: While this book focuses on Google, it is important that you add your business with each of these listed. By registering with each one, Google will look at your listing as being more relevant and trustworthy, which is very important in your rankings.

Step 4: You should now be at the Google Places page, which should look like something similar to this:

Google places

This is just a first step. Enter your business information here and watch your listing take shape on the right. In la service areas, and much more.

indicates a required field

Country: *	United States
Company/Organization: *	
Street Address: *	
City/Town: *	
State: *	Select state
ZIP: * [?]	

Note: You can hide your street address later if you don't want people to see it.

Main phone: *

Example: (201) 234-5678   Add more phone numbers

Email address:

Example: myname@example.com

Website:

Example: http://www.example.com

☐ I don't have a website.

Pacific Ocean

Top Rank Local

Chapter 5

Setting up Your Google

Places Listing

We will now get started into the strategy of setting up your Google Places listing for maximum effectiveness.

First, you will need to Sign-in with your Google account. If you do not have a Google account, you will need to create one. You can do that here:

https://www.google.com/accounts/NewAccount

After you log in, your next step is to click "Add New Business." Begin entering your business information into the text boxes. It is best not to leave anything blank, as we will discuss in greater detail later.

For the most part, setting up this listing on Google Places is relatively straightforward. You will need to list the country your business is located in as well as street address, telephone number, etc.

The important point I would like to make here when

entering this information is to keep it consistent with other information listed about your business online. If there is not much information online about your business, you will want to keep all future information you put online, consistent with your Google Places listing.

For example, if you list your telephone number as (619) 555-1212, do not list it elsewhere as 619-555-1212. If you list your business address as 223 Elm Street, do not list it elsewhere as 223 Elm St. If your zip code is listed as 90210-1101, do not later list it is 90210 (without the +4).

This consistency will help Google confirm that other mentions of your business online are, in fact, the same business as yours. And keep in mind that the more mentions of your business, the higher rankings you will get.

As you enter your business information, you will see the map move as it begins to find the location of your business as by the information you enter your business address.

DESCRIPTION

As mentioned, most of the information you will complete about your business is relatively straightforward. That is until you get to the description box. Here, I recommend a specific strategy involving the use of "keywords" relative to your business.

A "keyword" is a word or phrase that your customer uses to find you. For example, lets say my water heater blew up and was leaking water, I used the keyword, "Las Vegas Water Heater." Now, that may sound obvious, but what if you are an attorney practicing solely in Family Law? You do not want your description to read, "San Diego Attorney" but rather, you would want to focus on the keyword that your customers would use specifically to find you. In this case, I would likely use, "San Diego Family Law Attorney" as my primary keyword. But...I would expand on that to include other keywords as well. In this case, I would write something like this: "San Diego family law attorney practicing exclusively in child custody, child support, divorce and adoption." This way, I am hitting on other related keywords that deal with my profession, such as child custody, child support, etc. Google will put these keywords together and dish them out when your customer looks for you, but you need to do your part.

Now, that being said, it is important that you do not spam the "description" box. Many "newbies" coming along to set up Google Places listings often will resort to taking an approach similar to this: San Diego attorney, San Diego family law attorney, San Diego child custody attorney, San Diego divorce attorney, etc. In my experience, Google sees this as SPAM and you will be penalized rather than rewarded with a higher rank listing. It is important that your description reads like a coherent description of your business. And with a little effort on your part, you can nail the description and still use good keywords.

CATEGORY

In the "Category" box, you will enter your targeted keywords and keyword category phrases. For the most part, Google will attempt to find a matching keyword phrase for your business and this is fine just as long as the keyword suggestion actually matches that of your business. For the main category, Google now requires you to select at least one of their suggestions. But after that, you are free to type in your own category (Google allows five category listings).

If Google does not find a match for keywords that correlate to your business, you can "free text" your "category" yourself.

For example, if you happen to be a business that sells office cubicles and your customers find you by using the keyword phrase, "office cubicles" or "Seattle office cubicles" you will see that Google does not have a category for this. Instead, they will suggest the category of "Used Office Furniture Store." Obviously, this will not work as your primary category. If someone wants to purchase office cubicles, they are going to do a search for "cubicles" or "office cubicles" of "cubicle sales" etc.

Because Google requires you to use at least one of their suggestions, you will need to find the one that best matches what your customers would be looking for. Obviously, in the case of brand new office cubicles, the Used Office Furniture is not exactly the right category. So, instead you may want to use the Office Furniture category store or something similar.

After entering in your primary category, you will see that Google allows you to "add another category" with a link below the "category" box. Here, you can start using your own targeted keyword categories like "office cubicles" etc.

I highly recommend you add as many categories as possible. The more keyword targeted categories you use, the more chances you will get to have Google lead potential customers to you.

You can change this later, so do not fret if you find a better keyword to use later.

After completing the category section, you will click "Next" and you will be taken to a screen to complete even more details about your business.

The first one is:

SERVICE AREAS AND LOCATION SETTINGS

This is a new feature with Google as before, they did not offer traveling type businesses to expand their areas and list their business availability in other cities.

If you do have a business that travels to provide service in nearby areas, this is a great feature. Google will ask you to either give a service range in miles or you can list service areas by name. In this category, I prefer to list areas by name. And this is because if I am operating a plumbing repair business in Escondido and I list Escondido as my service area, there is the chance that if someone in Chula Vista type in plumbing repair, that my listing may show there.

The next categories will be specific to your business hours and methods of payments. These are pretty straightforward and again, I highly recommend that you do not skip any categories. Remember, we are trying to create the most RELEVANT listing possible.

PHOTOS

This is perhaps the most neglected category in setting up a listing on Google Places. But from my experience, photos help increase your relevance. And now that Google is offering a free photo shoot of your business, I think this category is more relevant than first imagined.

Google allows for 10 photos of your business. Is Google going to check to make sure photos of your law firm or pizza parlor are actually photos of your law firm or pizza parlor? No, of course not. But, Google will know that you have 10 photos, so be sure to upload all 1c photos here. Remember, you can always go back and do this later.

When you do upload photos to your Google Places listing, I highly recommend you naming those photos using keywords. For example, I would change the name of my photos on my computer before uploading to: san-diego-pizza.jpg, seattle-attorney.jpg, las-vegas-plumber.jpg, etc.

VIDEOS

Videos are utilized even less than photos because most businesses do not have or do not know how to make a video. I am going to offer a simple and free way to make a video for your business. And again, put as many videos as you can on your listing.

A simple, quick and free site to make a video for your Google Places listing is at *www.Animoto.com*. At this website, you can choose free video. They have music you can use as well as photos, etc. You can also upload your own photos to include in the video.

Animoto will make a cool looking 30 second video that you can upload not only to your Google Places listing, but also to YouTube. We will get more into this in a later chapter. For now, it is important that you work on getting your Google Places listing filled up and looking very RELEVANT to Google.

ADDITIONAL DETAILS

Here, you can again use your keywords where possible, but again, do not SPAM.

If I were an attorney, I may offer addition details like the type of law I practice. If I were a plumbing repair place, I may offer details about product names or repair services.

For example (attorney):

Family law: yes
Divorce: yes
Custody: yes

Example (plumbing repair):

Water heater repair: yes
Toilet repair: yes
Pipe replacement: yes

Continue to add these additional details until you have your keywords covered. I am not sure where the limit is on this, as I have never reached it. It appears that Google allows far more than 10 "details" so use as many as you need.

Keep in mind that the more you can use your main keyword, the better—but without spamming. For example, if you can use your keyword in your business name or website name, that will help with relevancy. I know this is not always possible, but something to think about when you are getting started.

You will now click the "Submit" button and Google Places will take you to a verification page. From here, you will be given the option to verify your Google Places listing by either telephone or by the business address you entered for your listing.

Telephone recommendation is highly recommended here as post card/mail verification takes 2-3 weeks. During telephone verification, Google will make an automated and immediate telephone call to you with a PIN number that you will have to enter into your Google Places listing. Once this is done, you will be verified and your business will be located on both Google Places and Google Maps! But...there is more work to be done because we aren't just looking for a listing...we are looking for a top listing that completely dominates your competition. With that, let's move on...

Chapter 6

Reviews

In my experience, reviews are an important fact in determining relevance with Google. The more reviews you can get for your business—the better.

But beware...

I've seen people get burned by trying to fool Google, by making up all kinds of fake reviews themselves. Understand that Google places "flash cookies" on your computer and they know who you are and where you are. Don't think for a minute that if you log out of one Google account and log back in with another that Google does not know it's you. They do know!

So, don't make the mistake that many do. Do not review your own business—at least not from any Google account that you have ever used on your computer in the past.

If you must review your own business, do it from a completely different computer, under a brand new account that has never been used by you...and use a computer outside of your home or business so the same IP address is not identified by Google.

An easy way to get reviews for your business quickly is to send an email. Google Places makes this easy.

To do this, go to your Google Places page and click on the link that reads, "See your listing on Google Maps." This will take you to your Google Maps listing.

Now, up in the right hand corner of your screen, you will see a picture of the map that depicts your business' physical location. Above that is links to print, email or get a link. If you click "email" a link containing your Google Maps listing will automatically show up in an email.

From here, you can send an email to your past clients, friends, family members or anyone that can give your business a review. They will need a Google Account (Gmail, etc) to do this, but it only takes a few minutes to make a Gmail account and to give you a review. If they already have a Gmail account, it will let them write a review right away.

Here's the email I send out. You can use this or alter it to suit your needs:

Hi <name>,

(Google.maps link here)

I have recently updated my business information on

Google and I would greatly appreciate it if you could visit the above link and write me a stellar review.

If you don't already have a Gmail account, you can set one up in under a minute.

I really appreciate your support!

This should get you some reviews. And with these reviews, your relevance with Google will begin to grow. Remember, the more reviews you can get—the better so be sure not to skip this.

Top Rank Local

Chapter 7

Google Services

I do not have any data on this whatsoever, but I have read that Google may attribute more relevance to you when you include their services.

COUPONS

One of these services is the Coupon function that is in your Google Maps page. I do suggest you include some type of coupon in your listing as it provides a webpage reference that adds authority to your business link.

Coupons are very easy to create. Basically, all you need to do is type in some text. If you want to get advanced and include a photo, this is easy to do as well.

To get to the Coupon function, you will see two options at the top of your Google Places page, #1 DASHBOARD and #2 COUPONS. All you need to do is click on the COUPONS tab and you will be brought to the page where you can make your coupon.

See screenshot example on next page:

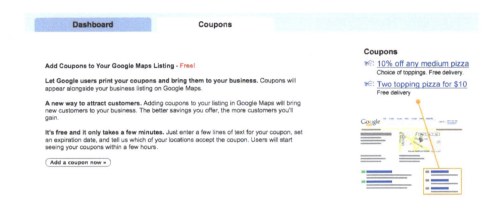

From here, you just need to click on the "Add Coupon Now" button and that will take you to the Coupon construction page.

From here, you just need to enter the information in the appropriate boxes and click "Continue." From there you will approve your coupon and it will go live.

GOOGLE CHECKOUT

Google Checkout is similar to PayPal in that it is an intermediary online payment processor. The SEO rumors are that Google will see your website as more relevant when you are using this service. And based on my study and what I have learned from other SEO experts, I do recommend using Google

Checkout if you can.

Google Checkout is listed as a payment option when you enter payment options in your listing. I suggest you go back to your listing and click on the "Google Checkout" box.

If you would like to add Google Checkout as a method of payment, you can set up a Google Checkout account at checkout.google.com.

USER DATA

Go to Google.com and click "Maps." For this example type in "Seattle gyms." On the left side (in the box), you will see a listing of gyms in Seattle. Click on the "more info" on one of those listings and it will take you to that Google Maps page. If you scroll to the bottom of the page, you will see "User Content." User content is information left that users have left in open collaboration. These Google users can add maps, reviews, photos, etc. The important feature here that I want to point out is adding a Map—basically, a map inside the map. I do not suggest you do this with your business Gmail account, however.

This feature will increase your relevance by showing that other people have "mapped" your location, usually indicating it is one of their favorite places. If you are a favorite among many, you will be a favorite to Google as well.

Here's how to add a map:

Go back to Google's Map page and sign in with an account that is not your business account.

Sign-in and click "Maps" then click again "My Maps" then click "Get Started".

What you want to do is create a map containing 'tagged' locations.

You can type in your business name and zip code and it will bring you to your listing.

Click the "Public Map" option then "Save".

Zoom-in the map at the location of your business listing. To add tags, click on the "tag" icon (the blue marker at the top of the map) and drag it to the right location on the map.

A window will appear for you to enter the "Title", type your business name in it. In the "Description" box, you can write any description you want but just be sure to include your business address and phone number just as it appeared in your Google maps listing. Then click "OK".

Your Google Maps listing will now display this user content you just added.

Get your customers, friends and families to do the same. This will help increase your relevance with Google.

Top Rank Local

Chapter 8

Becoming Relevant

Part of becoming more relevant to Google is by being trusted. Part of being trusted is being listed elsewhere on the Internet on websites that Google trusts.

To start earning this trust, you should begin by adding your business to other listing services in addition to Google. Google will cross-reference your information contained in other listings. When you list your business with other sites, you should include your address, phone number and all other information that is requested. And remember to keep this information consistent as stated earlier in this book, as you want each and every listing to look exactly alike so that Google counts that listing as being you and, in turn, ranks you higher.

Adding your business to other listings will move you up higher in Google's 7-box.

The websites that are included here are chosen because they are trusted by Google and also because they are FREE. I highly recommend that you register at each of these.

Yahoo

Go to *www.local.yahoo.com* and scroll to the bottom of the page. Click "Add a Business."

Enter your business information and click "Submit."

Info USA

Register and setup. Click "Add Business Record". Fill in the information required then click "Submit". Select your business classification. Be sure to enter the same information as the one you entered in Google Maps local listing. Click "Submit."

A message is displayed informing you that it will take up to sixty (60) days for the business to get listed.
Remember: the information you include in the other listings should be exactly the same information for each listing or as close to it as possible.

Bing

Go to *https://ssl.bing.com/listings/ListingCenter.aspx*

Click "Check Your Listing", type in your business information. If the listing is not found, you will be able to log in with a Windows Live ID account (hotmail, etc). From here you can enter your business information similar to what you did when you set up your Google Places listing.

Yellow Pages.com

Go to *http://listings.yellowpages.com*. Click "Get your Free Listing Now". Search for your business by entering your phone number. Since it's not yet on the list, you can enter your business information. Click "Continue" button.

Choose the nearest category for your business. Narrow it down to a more specific category if possible. Click "Add Category" for every category that you have chosen. You are allowed up to five categories to add. Click "Continue" button.

Enter additional information as close as the information from the other listings you've created. Enter the "Access Code" then click "Create Listing".
A new page will prompt you to create an account with yellow pages. Enter information and click "Register."

Super Pages

Go to *www.supermedia.com* and click "Free Business Listing" at the bottom of the page.

Enter your business phone number then click "Search." It's not yet on the list so click "Continue" button.

Enter your business information. From the "Choose Your Business Category", enter a category then click "Search."

Add all possible categories. There are no limits as to how many categories to add. Click "Continue" button if you're done adding categories.

Select as many products, services or brands that are applicable to your business. Enter your business hours, payment options, additional details, photos and coupon. Click "Preview". If you like to upgrade for better listing, you have to pay a certain fee. Click "No, Thanks" to continue if you're happy with the free listing.

A page prompts you to create your account. Fill-in the information then click "Sign-in". Enter your account details then click "Continue."

The "Order Page" appears. Just check the "I Accept" button below then click "Complete Order".
The "Order Confirmation" page appears confirming that the list has been added.

Local Eze

Go to *www.localeze.com* and click "List your Business Today." From there, go to "Sign Up" and enter your business information. Local Eze usually takes a few weeks before you are listed but this is one of my favorite resources.

Navteq

Register at *http://mapreporter.navteq.com/*. Enter your business address then click "Find". It's not on the list so click "Click to add a dragable place marker on the map". Drag the place marker to your desired location.
Fill-in the "Point of Interest" (POI) information, then click "Submit".

Yelp

Go *www.yelp.com* and click "Business Owner" at the bottom page. Click "Get Started."

Search for your business name. It's not there so you can now "Add your Business to Yelp". Fill-in your business information like what you did with the other listing services. Click "Submit."

Check your email to verify by clicking on the link provided.

City Search

Go to *www.citysearch.com* and search for your business name. If it wasn't found then click "Add Business." Enter your business information then click "Submit."

www.insiderpages.com
Go to *www.insiderpages.com* and search for your business name.

If it wasn't found then click "Add a Business". Click "Join Today" and fill your account and business information.

You can now "Claim this Business."

Other Directories

You can choose from other service listings below that are applicable to your business. The procedure is almost the same when adding a new business. Be sure to enter the exact information as those you have entered from the previous listings.

- *http://tripadvisor.com/*
- *http://gayot.com/*
- *http://ask.com*
- *http://guidespot.com*

- *http://zagats.com*
- *http://fodors.com/*
- *http://travelocity.com/*
- *http://wcities.com/*
- *http://hotelguide.net/*
- *http://merchantcircle.com*

Submit your business to as many listing services as possible so Google can find many references to your business online. This will give your business a better chance to appear in the 7-Box of its local listing.

After listing your business to several services, I recommend that you "social bookmark" all your business listings in each of these directories. Social Bookmarking is a way to publicly share your bookmarked websites and it is another way to make your business become more relevant in Google's eyes.

Start with *www.socialmarker.com*. Just have a copy of all your business listing URLs and bookmark it in as many social bookmarking sites as possible.

There are also paid listing services that remove the time and effort it takes for you to list your business at each individual site. My favorite is Universal Business Listings which can be found at *www.UBL.org.*

Here's what the UBL.org website says about handling this service for you:

Local Search Listing, Correction and Enhancement

The foundation of creating a business identity and marketing it is to first make sure the company's name, address, phone number and description can be found on Search Engines, online Yellow Pages, Social Networks, 411 Directory Assistance and Mobile/GPS navigation devices.

These local business searches are driven by databases of such listings, not from Website information. It is where 75% of all business searches take fewer experts know the tricks in dealing with 800-numbers, P.O. Box numbers and non-traditional phone lines.

These listings are becoming more important now that Search Engines and Mobile services deliver localized information based on knowledge of where you are when you conduct a Web search.

Sophisticated Web users know that you can submit listings directly to several of the larger Search portals, but this is time-consuming, complicated and few experts know all the places where the data needs to go. Unlike Web search, which is dominated by Google, searches for businesses are more likely to happen on other sites and Mobile phones. Even fewer experts know the tricks in dealing with 800-numbers, P.O. Box numbers and non-traditional phone lines.

Universal Business Listing provides a single entry point where you can create enhanced business profiles and for $30 a year that data gets distributed to all major outlets including:

- *Search Engines such as Google, Yahoo, Bing*
- *Online Yellow Pages (Superpages, Yellowpages, YellowBook)*
- *Social Networks such as MySpace*
- *Portals and Guides such as AOL MapQuest, CitySearch*
- *Cell Phones and Mobile (BlackBerry and iPhone)*
- *411 Directory Assistance*
- *In-Car GPS Navigation and Telematics such as OnStar*

UBL is effective because it feeds directly into such databases as infoUSA and Acxiom that are used as primary trusted sources by all major publishers. Listings from UBL are considered verified and are distributed to hundreds of sites directly and indirectly by this method.

In my opinion, UBL's service is well worth the $30 it costs!

Top Rank Local

Chapter 9

Geo Target Your Business

With Photos

You can further increase your relevance by uploading photos of your business on public photo sharing sites. Specifically, these photos will be placed on maps at your business location.

There are two sites that I recommend and I will walk you through getting started on each.

Panoramio

Go to *www.panoramio.com* and sign-in (Sign-up for an account if you don't have one). Click "Upload your photos".

Click "Browse" for every photo to be uploaded then click "Upload" at the bottom of the page.

After successfully uploading all the photos, enter the title, tags and comment with your business name, tags and address as it appear in the Google maps listing.

To map the photos, click "Map this Photo" then map it to your business address. Click "Search" beside the address box then "Zoom" to make sure the photo is in the exact location you want (You can drag it to your desired location if it's not positioned there).

Then click "Save Position."

Repeat the process for all the remaining photos. Once finished mapping the photos, click "Save" at the bottom of page.

Flickr

Go to *www.flickr.com*. You can either create a new account or you can sign-in with a yahoo account.

Click "Upload Photos & Videos" then click "Choose your Photos & Videos" to pick up photos to be uploaded.

Be sure to click the "Public" option button before hitting the "Upload" button below the page. Click "Add a Description" so you can enter your business name, address and tags the same as it is in the Google Maps Listing. Click "Save."

To map the photos, click a photo then click "Add to your

map" on the bottom right pane. Click "OK", choose the "Anyone" option button as your "Default Permission". When your map is displayed, click the dropdown arrow list at the bottom and choose "All your content" to display all your photos. Drag each photo to your targeted location.

Mapping photos on Panoramio or Flickr help by adding more content to your business listing in Google.

You can also Geo Target with webcams which will further add more content and more citations to your Google Places listing. But due to the fact that most businesses do not incorporate webcams, I will not go into the details. If you are interested in pursuing this, however, a good place to start is www.earthcam.com.

Top Rank Local

Chapter 10

Citations

In traditional SEO, inbound links are critical to ranking well on the search engines. However, with Google's local algorithm—the one that is used to populate the 7-Box, Google Places and Google Maps, it appears that links are not as important as they are in traditional SEO.

In a patent owned by Google: Authoritative Document Identification, Google indicates the importance of physical location and how they tie citations to local businesses (U.S. Patent application #20060149800):

> Abstract: A system determines documents that are associated with a location, identifies a group of signals associated with each of the documents, and determines authoritativeness of the documents for the location based on the signals.

The patent information is quite a read, but in there, Google identifies what a document is:

> "document," as the term is used herein, is to be broadly interpreted to include any machine-readable and machine-storable work product. A document may include, for example, an e-mail, a web site, a business

listing, a file, a combination of files, one or more files with embedded links to other files, a news group posting, a blog, a web advertisement, etc.

What this shows is that a "spiderable" link is not necessary for your business to receive a citation online. It now appears that a mention of your business online is enough to give you some attention from Google.

But, just like links, it appears that Google still places an importance on where the citation comes from. If a citation comes from the local Chamber of Commerce, it seems to carry more weight than if it comes from your sister's blog (although the blog will still hold some weight because volume is important too).

There are many ways to get your business listed aside from Google maps. The reason why you should get listed in many places as possible is that you achieve more citations.

Citations make your business popular. The more citations you have, the more popular your business becomes. SEO calls this link popularity. Google and other search engines take into consideration the number and quality of links you have when it comes to link popularity.

The idea is the same in local search. However, it's not the

links that are taken into consideration but instead, the mention of your business name in relation to your business location.

When Google finds that you are listed in other sites with the same business location, "trust" builds up and you become very relevant in its eyes.

Now, what you want to do is start getting your business and its location placed on local websites to increase the amount of citations you have with Google Places/Google Maps.

To do this, you should first do a Google search for business directory websites in your local area. For example, if you are a plumber in Seattle, do a search for "Seattle plumber directory" or "Seattle business directory" etc. From the search results for this term, you should find good ideas to list your website.

In most cases, these types of websites will have a place for you to include your business information. If nothing is available, send them a request through a "contact us" link on the website.

Google will give you some serious credit if you are located on important websites like the Better Business Bureau and your local Chamber of Commerce websites because these are considered authoritative and because they have built-in trust.

The drawback, however, is that these are often paid listings, although they are usually well worth the price you pay.

Remember to bookmark each and every webpage where your business is mentioned!

Chapter 11

Facebook

I don't think there is an off-page SEO book on the market that does not at least mention Facebook. The fact is, Facebook recently ousted Google as the number one most visited website. Because of that, Facebook is an important player online.

Although Facebook is widely considered to be used privately between friends and family, it is also a powerful way for businesses to connect more personally with their customers.

Facebook allows for Business pages and it is important that you start one for your business. Setting one up is fast, easy and painless.

If you have yet to get a Facebook account you may sign-up for one. It's easy and it's free. Once logged in, click "Advertising" at the bottom of the page. Click the "Pages" menu at the top of the page then click the "Create a Page" button at the right side of the screen.

Choose the type of your business; enter your business page name in the text box provided then click "Create Page."

If you need additional information, check out the help center. The help center has all the information you need about setting up your Facebook page.

To enter the basic information about your page, click the "View Page", click the "Info" tab then click the "Edit Information."

Once you have adjusted the settings, you can click "Save Changes." (Be sure to enter your information as it appears in your Google Maps Listing).

Also be sure to add your website and target keyword phrases.

When you are ready to publish your page, simply click "Publish this Page". (You can make additional changes by clicking "Edit Page"). You can now add pictures. Your location should match your Google map listing. The page name should also be the name you have on your Google map listing.

Chapter 12

Spying on Your Competition

To get a top ranking in the regular search results, one must have the most number of powerful incoming links. SEO calls it link popularity.

The same works with Google maps. To get to the top, one must have the most number of website citations.

The fastest and easiest way to determine how to beat your competition is by spying on their Google Maps listings and using that information to your advantage. Understand that they are not in the number one position by luck or happenstance. They are there because they are doing something that has made them appear to be more relevant than you in Google's eyes (their local algorithm).

Again, in almost all cases, it is simply the fact that they have more citations than you. But, volume is not always the case. Once again, they may have a few less citations than you, but they may be listed on websites that Google deems more authoritative. But, as a general rule, go after the volume and revise later.

To see where your competition is receiving citations, all you need to do is go to their Google Maps page and scroll down to the category listed as "More about this place." This is where the citations for that business are listed. From here, you can visit these pages where your competitors are listed and try to get your business listed as well.

There are instances wherein a keyword phrase, say "Beverly Hills' cosmetic surgery", returns the #1-Box result when searched in Google although there are only a few citations. What made it to the top? It's because it had more reviews than the other competitors. But if you keep an eye on the status of this keyword phrase everyday you will see that this will not stand in the #1-Box spot long because it does lacks citations.

There are competitors that stay on the top position of the 7-Box although they don't have that much information like reviews, hours of operations, photos and videos, and other business information. What made them to the number one position? It's because they have the most number of citations listed on the Internet with their business name, business location and business phone number. It is clear that it's these citations that got to them to the #1-Box or to the number 1 position in the 7-Box.

So what is the bottom line? Go get your citations. Be sure to visit the citations of your competition and get mentioned on the same sites. Once you are listed on all the same sites that your competition is, go get more citations...and keep getting them. Go get more reviews...and keep getting them.

Adding citations and reviews on a regular basis will propel you to the top of the Google 7-box and perhaps even give you the royalty status of a #1-Box...and continuing to work on it will keep the competition at bay. This is how you dominate your competition and garner a ton of website visits, telephone calls and more traffic for your business.

Top Rank Local

Chapter 13

On Page SEO for Local Business

While off page is more important to Local Search results rankings than on page factors, I think it is very important to devote a short chapter on the basics of on page optimization as it pertains to Local Search results.

On-page optimization should begin as traditional SEO begins...and that is by building relevance through location + keywords.

Keyword placement in your website should be considered a high priority and they should be used with a geographic slant.

Additionally, your full business name, address and telephone number should be placed on every page in your website.

There are many places where you can insert your target keyword phrase to optimize your site. It is always recommended that, at minimum, you include the primary target keyword phrase in the title of your website. It is also great if you can work your keyword phrase into your business name.

For example, if you are a cosmetic dentist, the most likely keyword term used to find you would be, "cosmetic dentist." If you were based in Seattle and your actual business name was Brite Smile Dentistry, you would want to use something similar to: Seattle Cosmetic Dentist, Mark Rogers DDS: Bright Smiles Dentistry. This way, your keyword is placed out in front and used as the business name. And with the example I gave, you could still include your actual business name.

Besides the business name and website title, you should also include your target keyword phrase in your website's headline, main body text, footer, title tag and meta tags.

If you do not know how to do this yourself, I highly recommend hiring a professional Webmaster with SEO experience. They will know exactly what you're looking for and they can take the necessary steps to handle your on-page SEO so you don't take the chance of mistakenly altering something you shouldn't.

Conclusion

This book is meant to be a resource that can be used over and over again. The strategies and tactics detailed inside have been tested and proven to work for our clients virtually without fail.

If you follow the steps and take action, you can sit back and watch as your business climbs the ranks of Google Maps results and dominates the competition.

Remember, relevance is the key. Make your business relevant to Google through useful information, reviews, citations and a fully optimized Google Places listing and Google will reward you with higher rankings.

I wish you the best of luck and much more new business with your new, top Google rankings!